J

MAPWORLDS
PEOPLE

©1996 Franklin Watts

First American Edition 1996 by
Franklin Watts
A Division of Grolier Publishing
Sherman Turnpike
Danbury, CT 06816

Library of Congress information on file.

ISBN 0-531-14362-7

Editorial planning: Serpentine Editorial
Design and typesetting: R & B Creative Services Ltd
Color origination: R & B Creative Services Ltd
Illustrations: Sallie Alane Reason

Photographic credits:
Chris Fairclough Colour Library: 8, 14, 27, 28, 29;
The Hutchison Library: cover (right), 9, 10, 14-15, 18, 19, 26, 30;
Trip: cover (top and bottom), title page, 6-7, 12, 17, 20, 21, 22, 23, 24, 25;
Zefa: cover (left), 11, 13, 16.

10 9 8 7 6 5 4 3 2 1
Printed in Great Britain

MAPWORLDS

PEOPLE

Molly Perham
and Julian Rowe

Illustrated by Sallie Alane Reason

FRANKLIN WATTS
A Division of Grolier Publishing
LONDON • NEW YORK • HONG KONG • SYDNEY
DANBURY, CONNECTICUT

CONTENTS

INTRODUCTION 6-7

CANADA AND
THE UNITED STATES 8-9

MEXICO, CENTRAL
AMERICA, AND THE
CARIBBEAN ISLANDS
10-11

SOUTH AMERICA 12-13

NORTHERN EUROPE 14-15

SOUTHERN EUROPE 16-17

AFRICA 18-19

RUSSIA AND THE FORMER
SOVIET STATES 20-21

THE MIDDLE EAST 22-23

SOUTH AND SOUTHEAST
ASIA 24-25

CHINA, JAPAN, AND THE
PACIFIC ISLANDS 26-27

AUSTRALASIA 28-29

THE POPULATION
EXPLOSION 30-31

INDEX 32

NORTH
AMERICA

PACIFIC
OCEAN

SOUTH
AMERICA

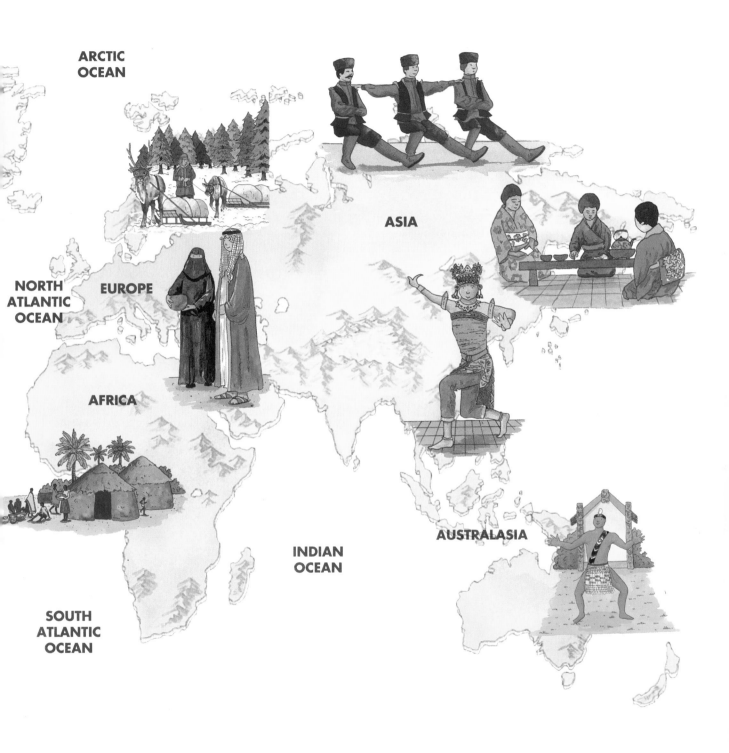

ARCTIC
OCEAN

ASIA

NORTH
ATLANTIC
OCEAN

EUROPE

AFRICA

INDIAN
OCEAN

AUSTRALASIA

SOUTH
ATLANTIC
OCEAN

INTRODUCTION

NORTH AMERICA

ATLANTIC OCEAN

SOUTH AMERICA

No ONE KNOWS for sure when manlike creatures first appeared on Earth, but modern humans first appeared in Europe and Asia around 35,000 years ago. From there they moved to America, crossing a piece of land that joined the two continents together. Early people were hunter-gatherers, moving around from place to place. Then they settled down to live in groups and to grow crops. From these settlements, the first towns and cities grew up.

People who have settled in different parts of the world have different life-styles, customs, and culture – and they even look different. For much of history, people have stayed in their native land, but during the past 300 years many have left to find work and homes in new countries. People from Europe and Asia moved to North America and Australia. Later, people from Africa and Asia emigrated to Europe. Today, most large cities have people from many different countries living and working in them.

In this book, look at the maps and pictures to see how people live all around the world.

• As a globe shows, the earth is round. A map is a drawing of the earth's surface on a flat piece of paper. On each page of this book an arrow shows which part of the globe is drawn flat on the map.

• At the bottom of each map there is a scale. The scale allows you to work out how far the real distance is between places on the map.

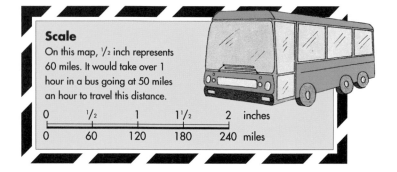

Scale
On this map, ¹/₂ inch represents 60 miles. It would take over 1 hour in a bus going at 50 miles an hour to travel this distance.

0	¹/₂	1	1¹/₂	2	inches
0	60	120	180	240	miles

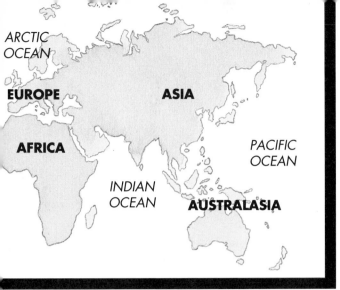

 • A compass tells you which direction is north, south, east, and west. There is a compass like this one at the top of each map.

Map symbols:

These picture symbols on the maps show religions and activities in selected places around the world.

Judaism

Christianity

Hinduism

Islam

Buddism

Shinto

Taoism/Confucianism

tribal religion

winter sports

tourism

forestry

commercial centers

fishing

nomads

industry

agriculture

◁ London has a multicultural population. People from the Caribbean, Africa, India, China, and many other parts of the world have settled in the city.

CANADA AND THE UNITED STATES

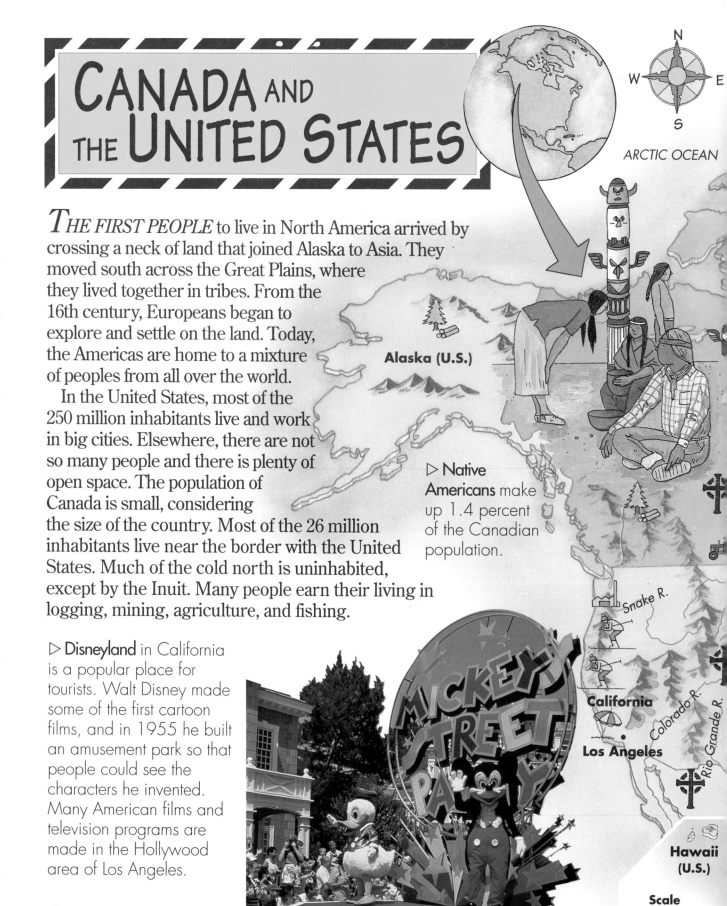

ARCTIC OCEAN

THE FIRST PEOPLE to live in North America arrived by crossing a neck of land that joined Alaska to Asia. They moved south across the Great Plains, where they lived together in tribes. From the 16th century, Europeans began to explore and settle on the land. Today, the Americas are home to a mixture of peoples from all over the world.

In the United States, most of the 250 million inhabitants live and work in big cities. Elsewhere, there are not so many people and there is plenty of open space. The population of Canada is small, considering the size of the country. Most of the 26 million inhabitants live near the border with the United States. Much of the cold north is uninhabited, except by the Inuit. Many people earn their living in logging, mining, agriculture, and fishing.

Alaska (U.S.)

▷ **Native Americans** make up 1.4 percent of the Canadian population.

Snake R.

California

Colorado R.

Rio Grande R.

Los Angeles

▷ **Disneyland** in California is a popular place for tourists. Walt Disney made some of the first cartoon films, and in 1955 he built an amusement park so that people could see the characters he invented. Many American films and television programs are made in the Hollywood area of Los Angeles.

Hawaii (U.S.)

Scale

0   ½   1

0   75   15[0]

8

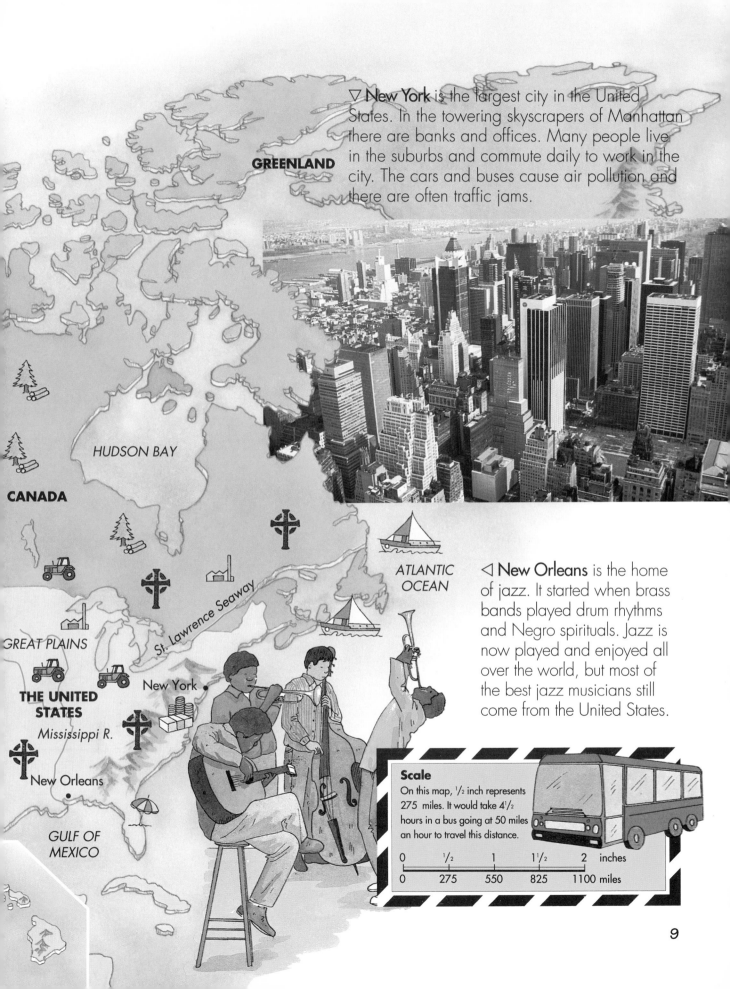

▽ **New York** is the largest city in the United States. In the towering skyscrapers of Manhattan there are banks and offices. Many people live in the suburbs and commute daily to work in the city. The cars and buses cause air pollution and there are often traffic jams.

GREENLAND

HUDSON BAY

CANADA

ATLANTIC OCEAN

St. Lawrence Seaway

GREAT PLAINS

THE UNITED STATES

New York •

Mississippi R.

New Orleans

GULF OF MEXICO

◁ **New Orleans** is the home of jazz. It started when brass bands played drum rhythms and Negro spirituals. Jazz is now played and enjoyed all over the world, but most of the best jazz musicians still come from the United States.

Scale
On this map, ½ inch represents 275 miles. It would take 4½ hours in a bus going at 50 miles an hour to travel this distance.

0	½	1	1½	2	inches
0	275	550	825	1100	miles

9

MEXICO, CENTRAL AMERICA, AND THE CARIBBEAN ISLANDS

IN 1492 Christopher Columbus discovered a "new world" across the Atlantic. Until then Europeans did not know that there had been civilizations in Central America for thousands of years. A Spaniard called Hernán Cortés took a small armed force to Mexico, destroyed the Aztec empire and claimed the land for Spain. Today, many people in Mexico and Central America are of mixed Spanish and Native American blood.

People from other parts of the world have settled in the Caribbean Islands. Spanish adventurers were followed by the Dutch, French, and English. They drove the native Carib and Arawak tribes off their land and planted sugar cane. Slaves were brought from West Africa to work on the plantations. Later, when slavery was abolished, workers from India and China replaced them. The descendants of all these peoples make up the present population.

MEXICO

Mexico City

△ **Mexico City** was built on the ruins of the great Aztec city of Tenochtitlán. It is one of the most crowded cities in the world, with a population of over 20 million. There are not enough jobs and houses for everyone, so poor people build shelters with anything they can find.

▷ **Carnivals** are lively and colorful events in Caribbean life. Each island celebrates in its own style, with street parades and dancing that last for several days. The main religion of the islands is Roman Catholic, and one of the most important carnivals is just before Lent.

ATLANTIC OCEAN

GULF OF MEXICO

CUBA

CARIBBEAN ISLANDS

DOMINICAN REPUBLIC

HAITI

JAMAICA

BELIZE

GUATEMALA

HONDURAS

EL SALVADOR

NICARAGUA

CARIBBEAN SEA

COSTA RICA

PANAMA

△ **Trinidad** is famous for its steel bands and calypso music. Steel drums were first made from scrap oil drums. The metal was beaten out so that a variety of notes can be played by striking different parts.

TRINIDAD & TOBAGO

▷ **Many Guatemalans** are descendants of the Maya, whose civilization lasted until the 9th century. The crafts of basket-making, pottery, wood-carving, and weaving are still practiced today.

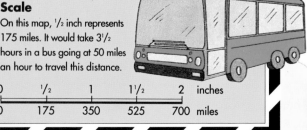

Scale

On this map, ¹/₂ inch represents 175 miles. It would take 3¹/₂ hours in a bus going at 50 miles an hour to travel this distance.

0	¹/₂	1	1¹/₂	2	inches
0	175	350	525	700	miles

SOUTH AMERICA

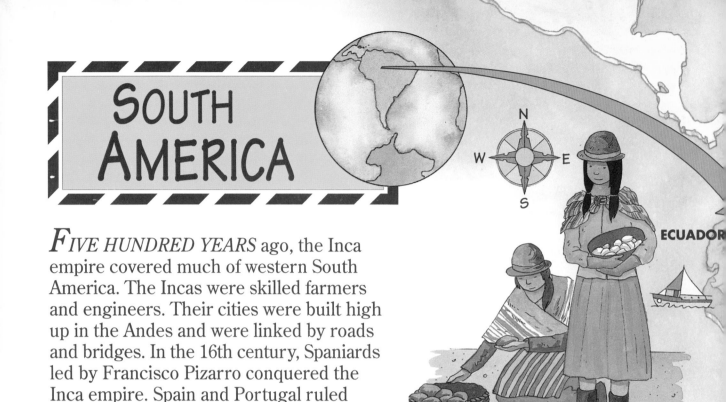

ECUADOR

PACIFIC OCEAN

FIVE HUNDRED YEARS ago, the Inca empire covered much of western South America. The Incas were skilled farmers and engineers. Their cities were built high up in the Andes and were linked by roads and bridges. In the 16th century, Spaniards led by Francisco Pizarro conquered the Inca empire. Spain and Portugal ruled most of South America for many years. Today, most of the people speak Spanish or Portuguese.

South America has rich farmland and huge amounts of oil and minerals. Mining is an important industry in Brazil, and Venezuela has a thriving oil industry. Despite this, many of the people in South America are very poor.

△ **Bolivia** is one of the poorest countries of South America. More than half of the population are native Indians, who live on farms in the mountains as they have done for centuries. The women wear distinctive bowler hats and colorful woolen blanke as protection against the cold.

▷ **The Amazon people** live in harmony with their surroundings, obtaining food by hunting and fishing, and by gathering fruits and roots. Some live in floating homes, or in houses on stilts, to protect themselves from the river's floods. The destruction of the rain forest for mining is destroying their traditional way of life.

12

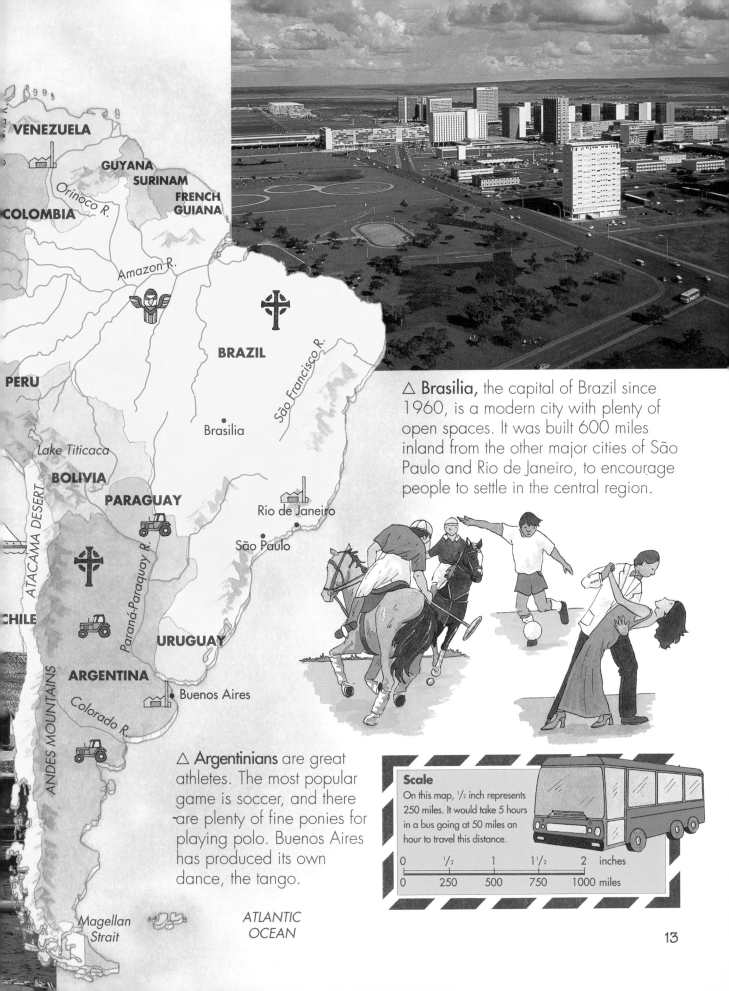

VENEZUELA

GUYANA
SURINAM
FRENCH
GUIANA

COLOMBIA

Orinoco R.

Amazon R.

BRAZIL

PERU

São Francisco R.

• Brasilia

Lake Titicaca

BOLIVIA

PARAGUAY

Rio de Janeiro

ATACAMA DESERT

Paraná-Paraguay R.

São Paulo

CHILE

URUGUAY

ARGENTINA

ANDES MOUNTAINS

Colorado R.

• Buenos Aires

Magellan Strait

ATLANTIC OCEAN

△ **Brasilia,** the capital of Brazil since 1960, is a modern city with plenty of open spaces. It was built 600 miles inland from the other major cities of São Paulo and Rio de Janeiro, to encourage people to settle in the central region.

△ **Argentinians** are great athletes. The most popular game is soccer, and there are plenty of fine ponies for playing polo. Buenos Aires has produced its own dance, the tango.

Scale
On this map, ½ inch represents 250 miles. It would take 5 hours in a bus going at 50 miles an hour to travel this distance.

0	½	1	1½	2	inches
0	250	500	750	1000	miles

13

NORTHERN EUROPE

ICELAND

MILLIONS OF PEOPLE live in the great capital cities of northern Europe. During the Ice Age, which ended about 10,000 years ago, there were very few people. When the ice sheets melted people from North Africa made their way through Spain to France and Britain and later to Norway and Sweden.

At different times in history, the people of Europe have either been united or at war. Two thousand years ago Europe was conquered by the Romans and united as part of their empire. In the 20th century Europeans have fought against each other in two world wars. Now, many countries belong to the European Union, but each has its own language and customs.

In parts of Britain, Germany, and the Netherlands, the population is dense and people live very closely together. Norway, Sweden, and Finland are together four times the size of Britain, but have only a quarter as many people.

N W E S

ATLANTIC OCEAN

SCOTLAND

NORTHERN IRELAND

IRELAND

WALES

ENGLAND

London

BELGIUM

Seine R.

FRANCE

Loire R.

▷ **The city** is the business center of London. During the day it is full of people who come to work by bus, train, or subway. At night the city becomes silent and empty when they return to their homes in the suburbs.

▷ **Cafés with tables** and chairs on the pavement are part of everyday French life. The café is where people meet to discuss business, play cards, enjoy a snack with friends, or just to read the newspaper while drinking a cup of coffee.

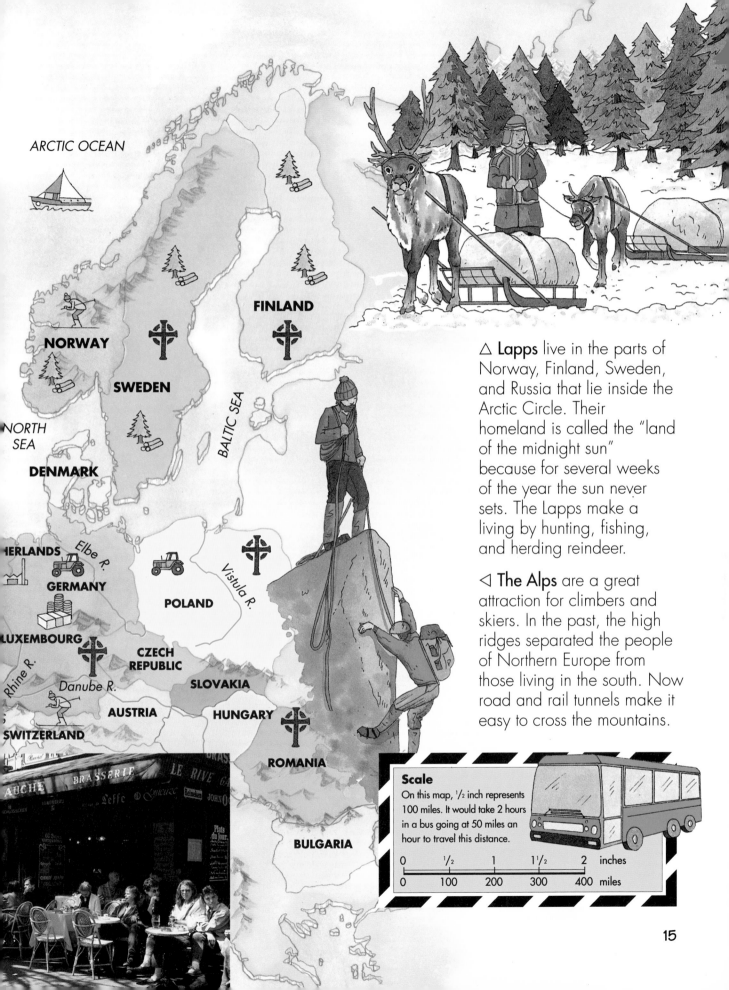

ARCTIC OCEAN

NORWAY

SWEDEN

FINLAND

NORTH SEA

BALTIC SEA

DENMARK

NETHERLANDS

Elbe R.

GERMANY

LUXEMBOURG

Rhine R.

Danube R.

SWITZERLAND

AUSTRIA

POLAND

Vistula R.

CZECH REPUBLIC

SLOVAKIA

HUNGARY

ROMANIA

BULGARIA

△ **Lapps** live in the parts of Norway, Finland, Sweden, and Russia that lie inside the Arctic Circle. Their homeland is called the "land of the midnight sun" because for several weeks of the year the sun never sets. The Lapps make a living by hunting, fishing, and herding reindeer.

◁ **The Alps** are a great attraction for climbers and skiers. In the past, the high ridges separated the people of Northern Europe from those living in the south. Now road and rail tunnels make it easy to cross the mountains.

Scale
On this map, ½ inch represents 100 miles. It would take 2 hours in a bus going at 50 miles an hour to travel this distance.

0	½	1	1½	2	inches
0	100	200	300	400	miles

15

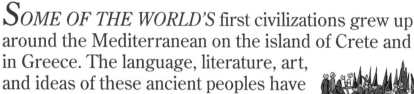

SOUTHERN EUROPE

SOME OF THE WORLD'S first civilizations grew up around the Mediterranean on the island of Crete and in Greece. The language, literature, art, and ideas of these ancient peoples have had a great influence on the way we live. Two thousand years ago, the Romans who lived in the country that we now call Italy took control of the Mediterranean. Their empire extended from the north of Africa across most of Europe. The city of Rome is the capital of modern Italy.

In the 16th century, Spain and Portugal were the two greatest powers in Europe. Adventurers explored other lands and both countries set up huge empires with colonies in Africa, America, and Asia.

Today Italy, Spain, Portugal, and Greece are independent countries with their own governments, languages, customs, and traditions. They all belong to the European Union, which helps industry, agriculture and trade through a "common market."

▷ **The Roman Catholic Church** plays an important role in the lives of most Spanish people. Nearly everyone is a member of the church and attends mass on Sundays. During Holy Week that leads up to Easter, processions take place in many towns and villages.

▷ **Italians** love the opera, theater, festivals, and dressing up. Venice is famous for its carnival, when everyone wears colorful masks and costumes.

SLOVENIA

CROATIA

BOSNIA-HERZEGOVINA

SERBIA

Po R. • Venice

Provence

ITALY

MONTENEGRO

MACEDONIA

ADRIATIC SEA

Rome

ALBANIA

GREECE AEGEAN SEA

BLACK SEA

TURKEY

MEDITERRANEAN SEA

CRETE

△ **Traditional crafts** are still practiced by villagers in many Mediterranean countries. In Crete wool is spun, dyed, and woven by hand into brightly colored rugs.

◁ **Boules, or petanque**, was first played in Provence and is now popular all over France. The game is played anywhere in the open air – in parks, on beaches, or in a back alley. The winner is the one who throws the boule nearest to the target ball, or jack.

Scale
On this map, 1/2 inch represents 100 miles. It would take 2 hours in a bus going at 50 miles an hour to travel this distance.

0	1/2	1	1 1/2	2	inches
0	100	200	300	400	miles

AFRICA

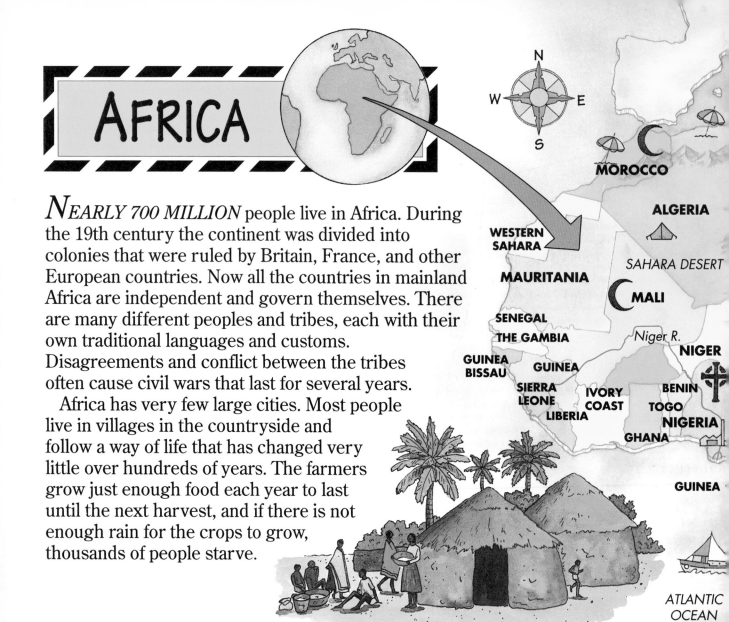

NEARLY 700 MILLION people live in Africa. During the 19th century the continent was divided into colonies that were ruled by Britain, France, and other European countries. Now all the countries in mainland Africa are independent and govern themselves. There are many different peoples and tribes, each with their own traditional languages and customs. Disagreements and conflict between the tribes often cause civil wars that last for several years.

Africa has very few large cities. Most people live in villages in the countryside and follow a way of life that has changed very little over hundreds of years. The farmers grow just enough food each year to last until the next harvest, and if there is not enough rain for the crops to grow, thousands of people starve.

MOROCCO

ALGERIA

WESTERN SAHARA

SAHARA DESERT

MAURITANIA

MALI

SENEGAL

THE GAMBIA

Niger R.

NIGER

GUINEA BISSAU

GUINEA

SIERRA LEONE

IVORY COAST

BENIN

TOGO

LIBERIA

NIGERIA

GHANA

GUINEA

ATLANTIC OCEAN

△ **In parts of East Africa** the villagers build huts of mud, which is then baked hard by the sun. The thatched roofs give shelter from the heat, and protection during the rainy season.

◁ **South Africa** has a large number of white inhabitants who are descended from British, Dutch, and German settlers. Until recently, white people controlled South Africa and its wealth. Many black Africans had to live in squalid "shanty towns" like this one outside Cape Town. Today, a new black government is hoping to improve housing.

TUNISIA

LIBYA

EGYPT Nile R.

SUDAN

CHAD

CENTRAL
AFRICAN
REPUBLIC

CAMEROON

Zaire (Congo) R.

GABON ZAIRE

CONGO

ANGOLA

NAMIBIA

BOTSWANA

SOUTH
AFRICA

Cape Town

LESOTHO

ZAMBIA

ZIMBABWE

MOZAMBIQUE

SWAZILAND

MALAWI

TANZANIA

Rift Valley

UGANDA

KENYA

ETHIOPIA

ERITREA

DJIBOUTI

SOMALIA

RED SEA

INDIAN
OCEAN

MADAGASCAR

△ **The Tuareg** are nomadic people of the
Sahara Desert. They live by herding
sheep and goats, moving their tents
around to find water and new pastures.

▽ **Ethiopia** is one of many African
countries that suffer from drought.
Often water has to be carried great
distances from the nearest river or
well. This boy is guarding pots
that hold precious drinking
water for his family.

Scale
On this map, 1/2 inch represents
300 miles. It would take 6 hours
in a bus going at 50 miles
an hour to travel this distance.

0	1/2	1	1 1/2	2	inches
0	300	600	900	1200	miles

RUSSIA
AND THE FORMER SOVIET STATES

*T*HE WHOLE OF THIS vast area used to be known as the Union of Soviet Socialist Republics, or U.S.S.R. In 1991 the Russian Federation, the Baltic States, Georgia, Belarus, Ukraine, and Moldova became independent republics, although most of them kept up their old links by forming a Commonwealth of Independent States (C.I.S.). Russia is the largest of the Commonwealth states, with a population of nearly 150 million. Russia is home to many different people. Some are Russian-speakers, while others have their own languages and traditions. Most people live in the west, in Moscow and other industrial cities. Much of Siberia is an empty wilderness.

Today Russia is going through great changes. When the U.S.S.R. was governed by communists everything was owned and run by the state. Now the government encourages people to own farms and businesses.

ARCTIC OCEAN

BARENTS SEA

ESTONIA
LATVIA
LITHUANIA
BALTIC SEA
Moscow
Volga R.
BELARUS
Dnieper R.
Don R.
UKRAINE
MOLDOVA
UZBEKISTAN
GEORGIA
BLACK SEA
AZERBAIJAN
ARMENIA

◁ **The Russian Orthodox Church** bases its beliefs on Christianity and the Bible. The churches are ornate, and topped by brightly colored domes. The priests wear costly robes and use incense during services.

▷ **Space exploration** is one of Russia's technological achievements. In 1961 the first Russian cosmonaut rocketed into space. Ten years later the first space station, *Salyut*, was launched.

◁ **Folk dancing** is very popular in Russia. Each region has its own dances, which are performed wearing colorful traditional costumes. The dances of south are marked by the remarkable agility of the male dancers.

KARA SEA

RUSSIA

Siberia

Yenisey R.

Lena R.

Ob R.

KAZAKHSTAN

KYRGYZSTAN

TAJIKISTAN

TURKMENISTAN

△ **The nomads** of central Siberia live in tents called yurts, which are made from skins stretched over a frame. These people still follow a traditional way of life, wandering with their herds and moving the yurts from place to place. However, many nomads have now settled down in towns.

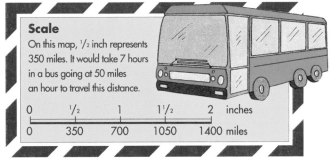

Scale
On this map, ¹/₂ inch represents 350 miles. It would take 7 hours in a bus going at 50 miles an hour to travel this distance.

0	¹/₂	1	1¹/₂	2	inches
0	350	700	1050	1400	miles

THE MIDDLE EAST

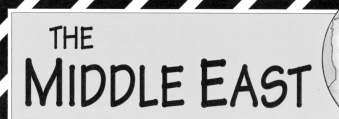

ONE OF THE FIRST civilizations in the world was in Mesopotamia, between the Tigris and Euphrates rivers. The Mesopotamians were the first people to plant crops and to domesticate animals. Their villages and towns developed into the first great cities. Today this is still one of the most fertile areas of the Middle East.

About three-quarters of the people in the Middle East are Arabs. Arabic is the main language and Islam the main religion. Judaism and Christianity also began here, and conflict among the three different religions has made the Middle East one of the most troubled areas in the world.

In recent years some countries of the Middle East have become rich from oil discovered deep underneath the desert. Saudi Arabia, the United Arab Emirates, and Kuwait are now among the richest countries in the world.

MEDITERRANEAN SEA

ISRAEL

Jerusalem •
GAZA STRIP
Suez Canal

Mecca

RED SEA

▷ **Jerusalem** in Israel is a holy city for Jews, Christians, and Muslims. The Wailing Wall is the last remaining part of the Temple of Herod, and is the Jewish faith's most holy place. Jews come to the wall to pray.

△ **Mecca** in Saudi Arabia is an important place for Muslims. It is the birthplace of their prophet, Muhammad. The Kaaba is Islam's holiest shrine. Muslims pray five times a day, and they always kneel in the direction of Mecca.

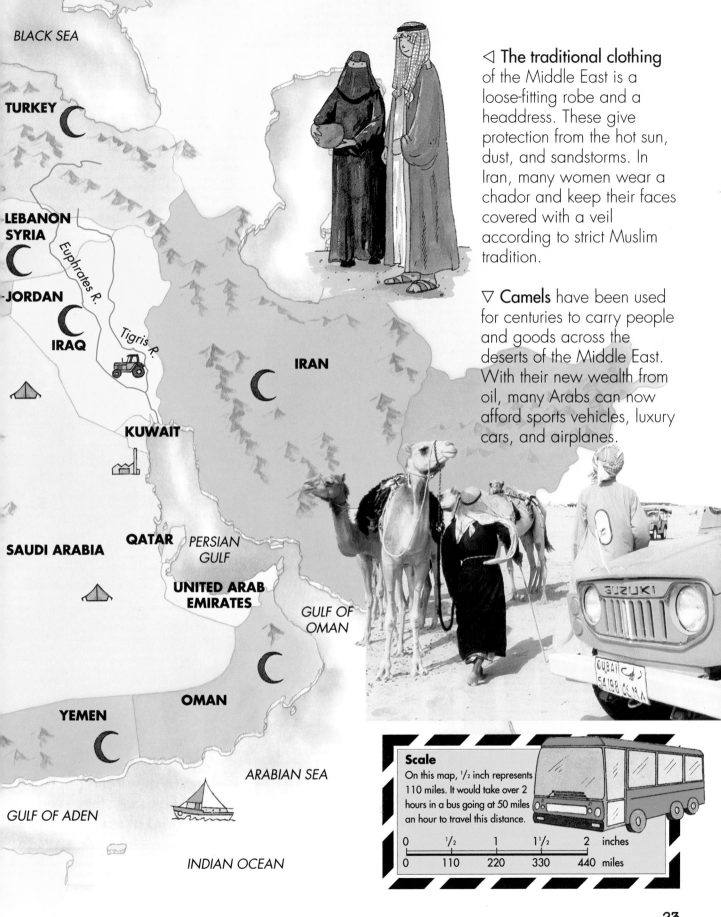

BLACK SEA

TURKEY

LEBANON
SYRIA

Euphrates R.

JORDAN

Tigris R.

IRAQ

IRAN

KUWAIT

SAUDI ARABIA

QATAR

PERSIAN
GULF

UNITED ARAB
EMIRATES

GULF OF
OMAN

OMAN

YEMEN

ARABIAN SEA

GULF OF ADEN

INDIAN OCEAN

◁ **The traditional clothing** of the Middle East is a loose-fitting robe and a headdress. These give protection from the hot sun, dust, and sandstorms. In Iran, many women wear a chador and keep their faces covered with a veil according to strict Muslim tradition.

▽ **Camels** have been used for centuries to carry people and goods across the deserts of the Middle East. With their new wealth from oil, many Arabs can now afford sports vehicles, luxury cars, and airplanes.

Scale
On this map, 1/2 inch represents 110 miles. It would take over 2 hours in a bus going at 50 miles an hour to travel this distance.

0	1/2	1	1 1/2	2	inches
0	110	220	330	440	miles

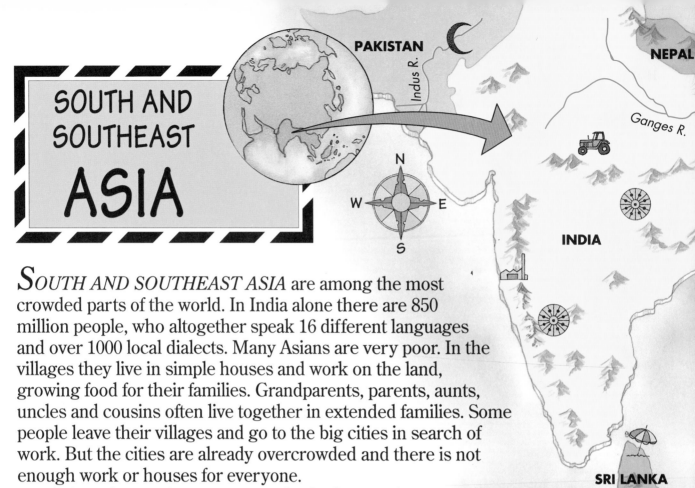

SOUTH AND SOUTHEAST ASIA

PAKISTAN

Indus R.

NEPAL

Ganges R.

INDIA

SRI LANKA

*S*OUTH AND SOUTHEAST ASIA are among the most crowded parts of the world. In India alone there are 850 million people, who altogether speak 16 different languages and over 1000 local dialects. Many Asians are very poor. In the villages they live in simple houses and work on the land, growing food for their families. Grandparents, parents, aunts, uncles and cousins often live together in extended families. Some people leave their villages and go to the big cities in search of work. But the cities are already overcrowded and there is not enough work or houses for everyone.

Religion plays an important part in the lives of Asian people. The majority of the people are Hindus, who believe in a supreme being called Brahma. Muslims follow the religion of Islam. They believe in one God, called Allah, and in his prophet, Muhammad. Pakistan and Bangladesh are mainly Muslim countries. Other religious groups are Sikhs, Jains, Buddhists, and Christians.

◁ **Buses** are so crowded in this region that people ride on the roof. Small carts called rickshaws are also a popular form of transport. They used to be pulled along by hand, but today cycles or motor scooters are used.

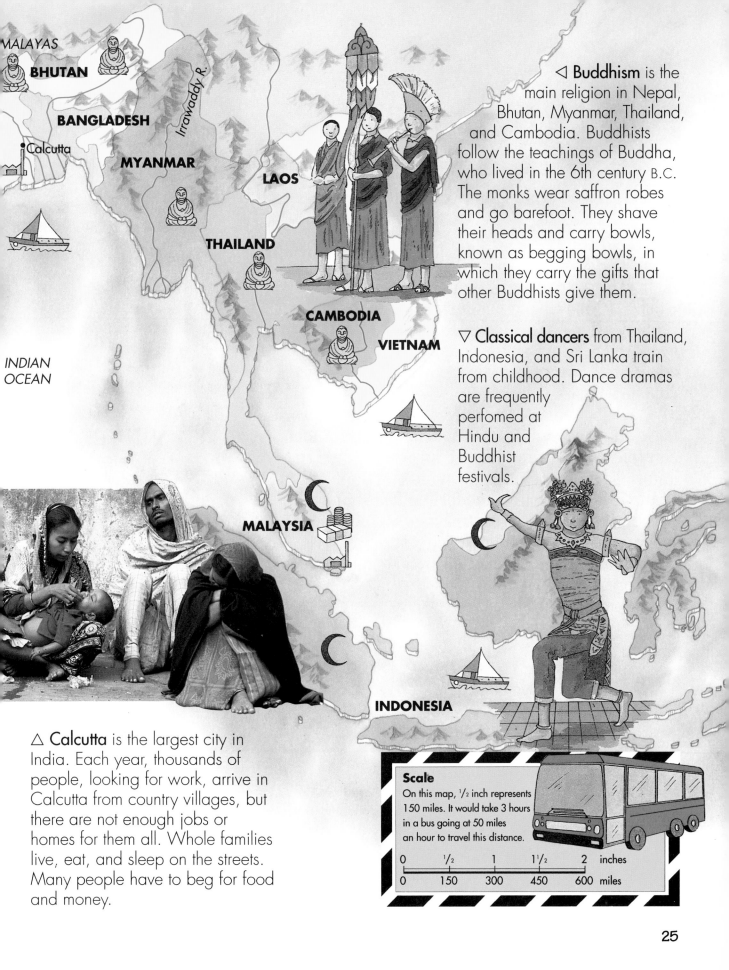

MALAYAS

BHUTAN

BANGLADESH

Calcutta

MYANMAR

Irrawaddy R.

LAOS

THAILAND

INDIAN OCEAN

CAMBODIA

VIETNAM

◁ **Buddhism** is the main religion in Nepal, Bhutan, Myanmar, Thailand, and Cambodia. Buddhists follow the teachings of Buddha, who lived in the 6th century B.C. The monks wear saffron robes and go barefoot. They shave their heads and carry bowls, known as begging bowls, in which they carry the gifts that other Buddhists give them.

▽ **Classical dancers** from Thailand, Indonesia, and Sri Lanka train from childhood. Dance dramas are frequently perfomed at Hindu and Buddhist festivals.

MALAYSIA

INDONESIA

△ **Calcutta** is the largest city in India. Each year, thousands of people, looking for work, arrive in Calcutta from country villages, but there are not enough jobs or homes for them all. Whole families live, eat, and sleep on the streets. Many people have to beg for food and money.

Scale

On this map, ½ inch represents 150 miles. It would take 3 hours in a bus going at 50 miles an hour to travel this distance.

0	½	1	1½	2	inches
0	150	300	450	600	miles

1416-3495

CHINA, JAPAN AND THE PACIFIC ISLANDS

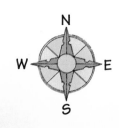

MORE THAN ONE BILLION people, one fifth of the world's population, live in China. Most of them are crowded together in the valleys of the Huang He and Chang Jiang rivers. Until the 20th century, China was ruled by emperors who allowed few foreigners to visit the country. In 1949 a communist government took power and began to change China.

Japan also remained isolated from the rest of world for a long time. A military dictator called the shogun controlled the country, helped by powerful warriors known as the samurai. In the middle of the 19th century, Japan began to modernize and soon became a successful industrial nation. Today, Japan makes more motor vehicles than any other country, and exports electrical goods all over the world.

▽ **Chinese farmers** grow rice and wheat, and raise pigs and other livestock. Most farmers have very little machinery and still use traditional methods.

◁ **Hong Kong** is an important financial center. It is heavily populated and its busy harbor is crowded with a floating "city" of boats. The boat people sell goods to the many people who visit Hong Kong.

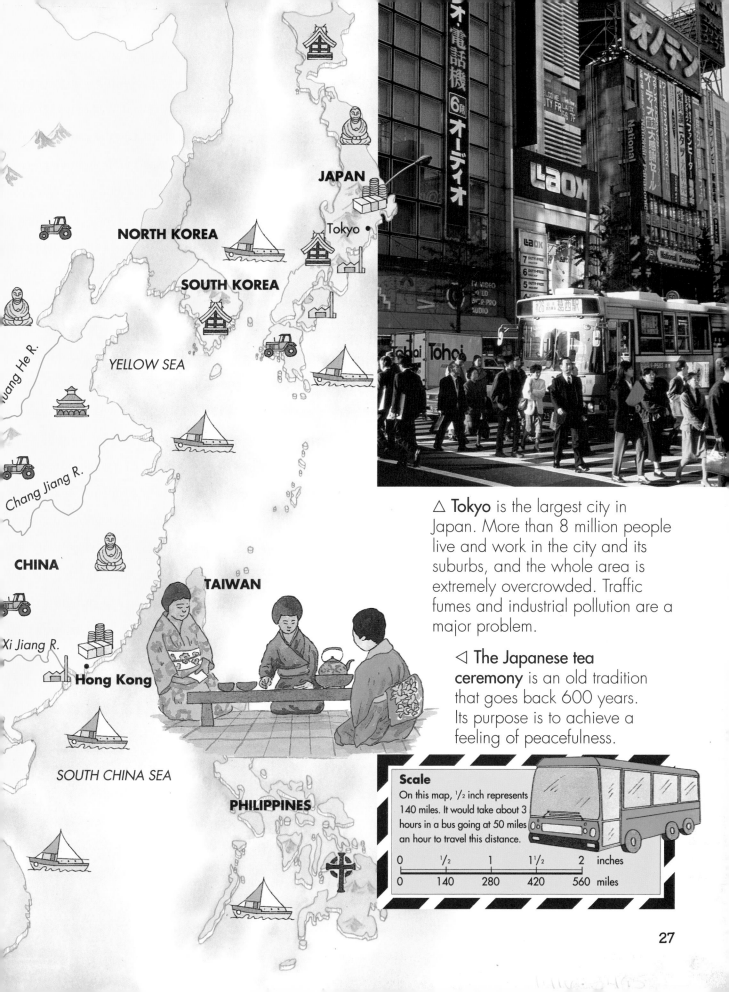

JAPAN

NORTH KOREA

SOUTH KOREA

Tokyo •

YELLOW SEA

uang He R.

Chang Jiang R.

CHINA

TAIWAN

Xi Jiang R.

Hong Kong

SOUTH CHINA SEA

PHILIPPINES

△ **Tokyo** is the largest city in Japan. More than 8 million people live and work in the city and its suburbs, and the whole area is extremely overcrowded. Traffic fumes and industrial pollution are a major problem.

◁ **The Japanese tea ceremony** is an old tradition that goes back 600 years. Its purpose is to achieve a feeling of peacefulness.

Scale
On this map, ½ inch represents 140 miles. It would take about 3 hours in a bus going at 50 miles an hour to travel this distance.

0	½	1	1½	2	inches
0	140	280	420	560	miles

AUSTRALASIA

MOST AUSTRALIANS live in the towns and cities on the east and southeast coast. Not many people live in the dry interior of the country, which is called the outback. The first inhabitants of Australia, the Aborigines, have lived there for 40,000 years. While some of them still follow a traditional life in the outback, hunting and gathering in small groups, many now prefer to live in the cities. Most of the first European settlers in Australia came from the United Kingdom, starting in the 17th century.

The original inhabitants of New Zealand, the Maoris, came from islands in the Pacific Ocean more than 1000 years ago. They settled down to farm the land in both the North and South Islands. Today Maoris mostly live in cities. Europeans began to settle in New Zealand at the beginning of the 19th century.

INDIAN OCEAN

AUSTRALIA

NULLABOR PLAIN

◁ **The Flying Doctor** service provides medical help for people in the outback. They can obtain advice by radio, or a doctor can fly to a remote ranch.

▷ **Aborigines** believe that the world was created by their ancestors during a period called Dreamtime. Paintings of the people, spirits, and animals of Dreamtime cover sacred cliffs and rocks in their tribal territories.

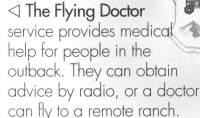

PACIFIC
OCEAN

▽ **Sydney** is the oldest and largest city in Australia. It was built around a huge natural harbor, and is a busy seaport and industrial center. The harbor is famous for its spectacular bridge and the unusual shell-shaped opera house.

PAPUA NEW
GUINEA

GREAT BARRIER REEF

Lake Eyre

Darling R.

Murray R.

Sydney

CORAL SEA

NEW ZEALAND

◁ **The Maori haka** is a traditional dance in which the participants pull exaggerated expressions of aggression or welcome. The dancers paint their faces and wear traditional skirts called piupiu. These are made from the leaves of a flaxlike plant and dyed in a bright pattern.

Scale
On this map, ½ inch represents 250 miles. It would take 5 hours in a bus going at 50 miles an hour to travel this distance.

0	½	1	1½	2	inches
0	250	500	750	1000	miles

29

THE POPULATION EXPLOSION

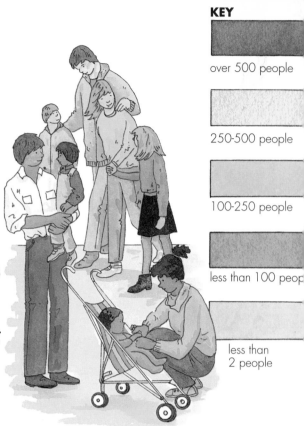

IN THE NEXT 50 YEARS, the number of people in the world will double. By the end of the century there will be more than 6 billion people. In the Middle Ages, it took 300 years for the number of people to double. The time it takes the population to double gets shorter and shorter: this is called the population explosion.

In the Americas and Europe, about 7 people in 10 live in cities. In the last century all the really big cities were in the northern hemisphere. Now the most rapidly growing cities are in Africa, Asia, and in South America. More than 70 cities have over a million inhabitants. Mexico City has 20 million.

◁ In some countries, families have as many as 6 or 8 children so that the population is growing very fast. In China the government has said that each family may have only one child. This is called the One Child Policy. But even if the plan works, it will be the next century before the population stops increasing.

1500   **1550**   **1600**   **1650**   **170**

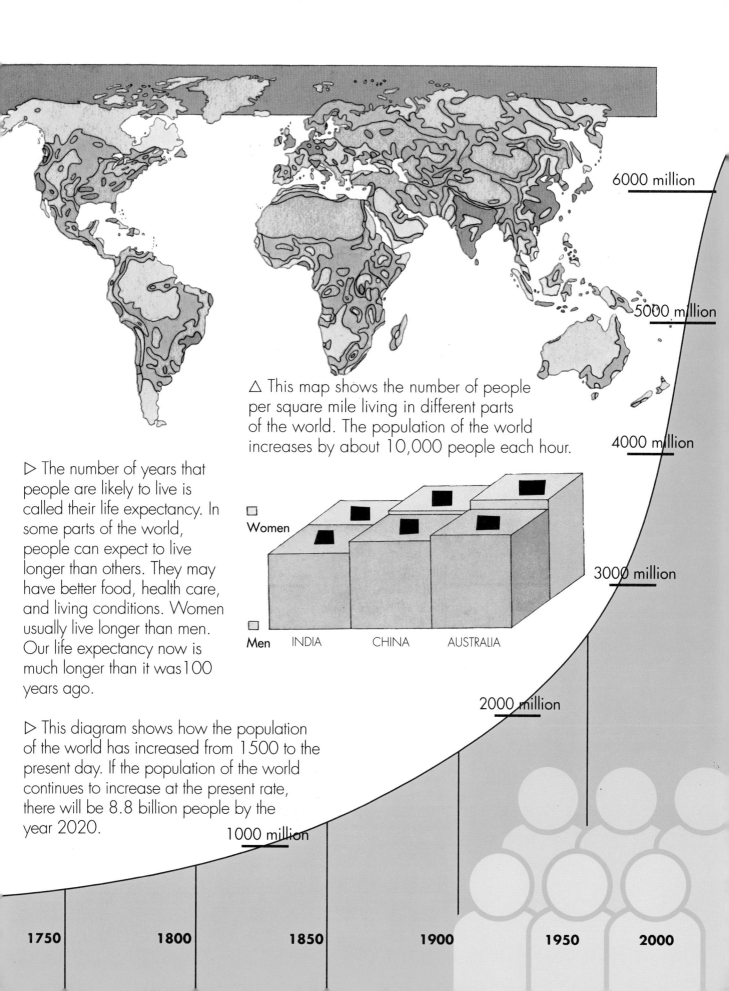

△ This map shows the number of people per square mile living in different parts of the world. The population of the world increases by about 10,000 people each hour.

▷ The number of years that people are likely to live is called their life expectancy. In some parts of the world, people can expect to live longer than others. They may have better food, health care, and living conditions. Women usually live longer than men. Our life expectancy now is much longer than it was 100 years ago.

▷ This diagram shows how the population of the world has increased from 1500 to the present day. If the population of the world continues to increase at the present rate, there will be 8.8 billion people by the year 2020.

Women

Men   INDIA   CHINA   AUSTRALIA

6000 million

5000 million

4000 million

3000 million

2000 million

1000 million

1750   1800   1850   1900   1950   2000

Index

Aborigines 28
air pollution 9
Alps 15
Amazon 12
Andes 12
Arabs 22
Arawak people 10
Arctic Circle 15
Aztecs 10

basket-making 11
boules 17
Brasilia 13
Buddhism 24, 25
Buenos Aires 13
buses 24

cafés 14
Calcutta 25
calypso music 11
camels 22
Carib people 10
carnivals 11, 17
Christianity 20, 22, 24
cities 6, 8, 9, 10, 13, 14, 24,
    26, 27, 28, 30
civil wars 18
civilizations 16, 22
clothes 22
colonies 18
Columbus, Christopher 10
common market 16
Commonwealth of Independent
    States (C.I.S.) 20
communism 20, 26
conquerors 10, 12, 14
Cortés, Hernán 10
Crete 16, 17

dancing 13, 21, 25, 29
Disneyland 8
Dreamtime 28
drought 19

education 26
European Union 14, 16
explorers 8, 10, 16
extended families 24

farming 18, 22, 24, 26, 28
flying doctor 28

government 20, 26
Great Plains 8

health care 26, 28
Hindus 24
Hong Kong 26
houses 10, 18, 24
hunter-gatherers 6, 28

Ice Age 14
Incas 12
Inuit 8
Islam 22, 24

Jains 24
jazz 9
Jerusalem 22
Judaism 22

Kaaba 22

languages 24
Lapplanders 15
life expectancy 30
London 14

Maoris 28, 29
Maya 11
Mecca 22
Mediterranean 16
Mesopotamia 22
Mexico City 10
Muslims 22, 24

native Americans 8, 12
New Orleans 9
New York 9
nomads 19, 21

oil 22, 23
One Child policy 30
outback 28

Pizarro, Francisco 12
plantations 10
population 10, 14, 20, 24, 30-
    31
pottery 11

religion 11, 24
Roman Catholic Church 11, 16
Romans 14, 16
Russian Orthodox Church 20

Sahara Desert 19
samurai 26
shanty towns 18
shogun 26
Siberia 20, 21
Sikhs 24
slaves 10
space exploration 20
sports 13
steel bands 11
suburbs 14, 27
Sydney 29

tea ceremony 27
Tenochtitlán 10
Tokyo 27
traditional costume 21
Tuareg 19

U.S.S.R. 20

Venice 17

Wailing Wall 22
water 19
weaving 11, 17
world war 14

yurts 21